Other books by **ANN BISHOP**

Chicken Riddle
The Ella Fannie Elephant Riddle Book
Hey, Riddle Riddle!
Merry-Go-Riddle
Noah Riddle?
Oh, Riddlesticks!
Riddle Ages
A Riddle-iculous Rid-Alphabet Book
Riddle Raddle, Fiddle Faddle
Riddle Red Riddle Book
Wild Bill Hiccup's Riddle Book

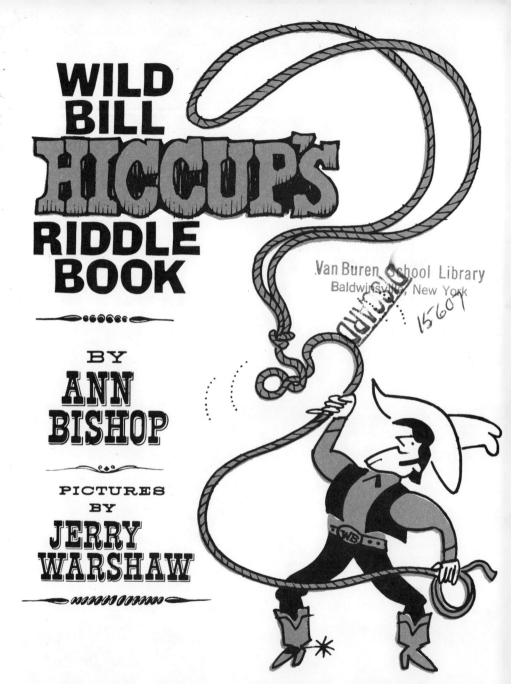

WILD BILL HICCUP'S RIDDLE BOOK

BY
ANN BISHOP

PICTURES
BY
JERRY WARSHAW

ALBERT WHITMAN & Company

Third Printing 1979

Illustrations © 1975 by Albert Whitman & Company
Published simultaneously in Canada by
George J. McLeod, Limited, Toronto
Printed in U.S.A. All rights reserved.

Flip the pages and see the action.

Library of Congress Cataloging in Publication Data
Bishop, Ann.
    Wild Bill Hiccup's riddle book.

    SUMMARY: A collection of riddles involving cowboys,
cattle, and other western themes.
    1. Riddles—Juvenile literature. [1. Riddles]
I. Warshaw, Jerry. II. Title.
PN6371.5.B54   398.6   75-33161
ISBN   0-8075-9097-5

This is Wild Bill Hiccup.

Why does Wild Bill Hiccup wear
such big boots?

What's Wild Bill Hiccup's favorite
color?

Because of his amazing feats.
Burple.

What is the name of Wild Bill
Hiccup's ranch?

What is its brand?

El Rancho Riddle.
???—The Triple Question Mark.

What does Wild Bill raise on
El Rancho Riddle?

Is there a lot of money to be
made in the cattle business?

Lots of things. His hat to his head, his
fork to his mouth—and cattle.
So I've herd.

This is Annie O'Kay.

Why are the clouds like Annie O'Kay
on a horse?

Because they hold the rains (reins).

When did Annie O'Kay have a hair-raising experience?

Where does she go when she wants a very small drink of pop?

Some people thirst after knowledge, some after money. What does Annie O'Kay thirst after?

What did Wild Bill Hiccup say when Annie O'Kay told him to shoo the flies?

When she ran a rabbit farm.
To mini-soda (Minnesota).
Salted nuts.
"Ah, let them go barefoot!"

This is Goldbrick, Wild Bill Hiccup's horse.

How did Goldbrick's ancestors come to America?

How could Goldbrick run all day and still move only four feet?

On the Hayflower.
That's all he has.

What happens when Goldbrick gets
to the bottom of his nosebag?

What's the principle part of a horse?

How do you know that Goldbrick is
polite?

It's the last straw.
The mane part.
When he comes to a fence, he lets Wild
    Bill go over first.

This is Fryem Frank, the cook.

What does Fryem Frank serve for breakfast?

Why is Fryem Frank the richest man on the ranch?

Riddle cakes.
He's got all the dough he kneads and lots of bread.

What tastes better before Fryem Frank cooks it?

Why does the coffee taste like mud?

What happened when Fryem Frank crossed a potato with a sponge?

Burnt toast.
It was just ground this morning.
He got a potato that tasted awful but
   held a lot of gravy.

This is Dandy Dudley, the Dude.

What did Dandy Dudley say when he found some milk cartons in the grass?

What did he do when Annie O'Kay told him to make his own bed?

How did the Dude burn himself?

What did Dandy Dudley think was the hardest thing about learning to ride a horse?

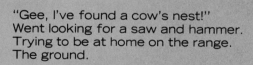

"Gee, I've found a cow's nest!"
Went looking for a saw and hammer.
Trying to be at home on the range.
The ground.

Here are the cowboys—
Slim, Shorty, and Yippie.

Do the cowboys go to bed with the
chickens?

How many boards went into building
the bunkhouse?

No, they sleep in the bunkhouse.
None. They all had to be carried.

What is Slim doing when he sleeps
soundly?

Why did Yippie put his bed
in the fireplace?

Which cowboy is the ringleader?

Snoring.
He wanted to sleep like a log.
The first one in the bathtub.

Why do the cowboys wear the brims
of their hats turned up?

What is a fillibuster?

What is bronchitis?

So three of them can ride in a pickup
  truck.
A cowboy who breaks in young mares.
An ailment cowboys get from riding
  wild horses.

What is a cowboy, anyway?

What is laughing stock?

What do you call a cow that sits on the grass?

A critter-sitter.
Cattle with a sense of humor.
Ground beef.

What's a tin of corned beef?

What's a baby cow called?

What did the absent-minded cow give?

An armored cow.
Condensed milk.
Milk of amnesia.

What did the bull say when he swallowed the bomb?

What did the calf say when it looked at the silo?

What did one cow say to the other cow?

"Abominable." (A bomb in a bull.)
"Is my fodder there?"
"Did you see the moo-vie last night?"

What kind of hot dogs does Fryem
Frank serve in winter?

How could Dandy Dudley have
breakfast without getting up?

How did Fryem Frank get fat?

Chili dogs.
He took a couple of rolls in bed.
He bought it from the butcher.

Why did Fryem Frank bring smashed doughnuts to the table?

Why didn't Annie O'Kay tell Wild Bill about the 5000-pound doughnut?

Because Wild Bill said he wanted a cup of coffee and a doughnut, and step on it! She knew he'd never swallow it.

Why did the turkey cross the road?

What did the baby chick say to his
mother when he couldn't get out of
his shell?

To prove he wasn't chicken.
"You got me into this—now get me out."

Why were the chickens dressed up?

How do hens and roosters dance?

What did the Spanish farmer say to his hen?

They were going to the fowl ball.
Chick to chick.
"Olé!" (Oh, lay!)

Shorty had two-and-a-half piles of oats in one barn and one-and-a-half piles in another. He put them together. How many piles did he have then?

What beats riding a horse across the desert at sixty miles an hour?

One.
Your heart, usually.

What did the pony say when he coughed?

Why is Goldbrick hard to get along with?

What's most like a horse, but isn't a horse?

"Excuse me—I'm just a little hoarse."
He is always saying, "Neigh."
A mare.

How do you hire a horse?

What did Goldbrick say when someone cut off his tail?

Put four bricks under him.
It won't be long now.

How can you make a slow horse fast?

How can you put a horse on his mettle?

What did the Dude say when Annie told him he put his horse's saddle on backwards?

Tie him up.
Shoe him.
"You don't even know which way I'm going!"

What did Goldbrick do when he wanted to go one way and the Dude wanted to go another?

What did the Texan say when the Dude asked him for change for a twenty-dollar bill?

Why did the Dude sleep under the old car?

What happened to Dandy Dudley when he tickled a mule?

Why didn't Dandy Dudley believe a lasso was used to catch cattle?

He tossed him for it.
"Fella, around here, a twenty IS change."
He wanted to get up oily (early).
He got a kick out of it.
He couldn't find any bait on the end of it.

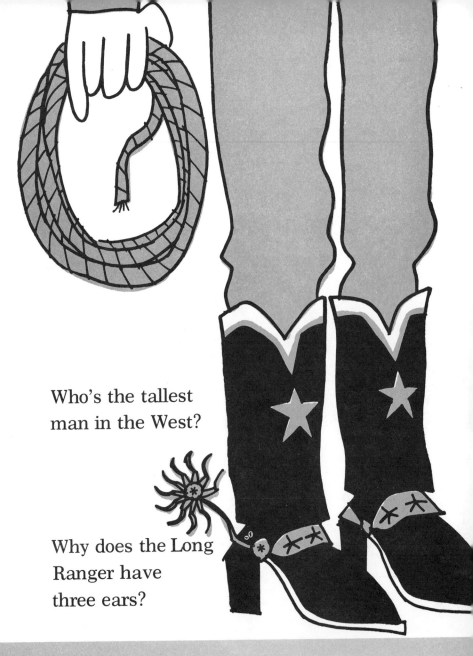

Who's the tallest
man in the West?

Why does the Long
Ranger have
three ears?

The Long Ranger.
Left ear, right ear, and wild frontier.

How do you know which beach towel belongs to the Long Ranger?

Wouldn't there be a lasso on it, too?

What did the Long Ranger do when his blanket was too short?

What did Annie O'Kay say when Yippie told her the Long Ranger's bed was twenty-five feet long and ten feet wide?

By the spurs lying on it.
Of course not! Who takes a lasso to the
    beach?
He cut some off the top and sewed it to
    the bottom.
"That's a lot of bunk!"

What well-known bandleader received
$100,000.00 in one minute?

Jesse James.

What happened when Slim fell
backward into the campfire?

When Shorty saw a kangaroo, what
did he think it was?

Why did the cowboys put blinker lights
on their saddle for night roundups?

What did Yippie say when the Dude
asked how he was doing with his
woodcarving?

He burned his britches behind him.
A Texas grasshopper.
They wanted to have communication
    saddle lights (satellites).
"It's coming along, whittle by whittle."

What was the Dude doing, leaning over a river, holding a fishing line?

Why did he throw away the big fish he caught and keep the little one?

Teaching a worm to swim.
His frying pan was only eight inches across.

Why does Wild Bill Hiccup wear loud socks?

When was Wild Bill afraid to go home because there was a masked man waiting for him?

What makes Wild Bill so hard-boiled?

To keep his feet awake.
When he was on third base during a
    baseball game.
He's been in hot water so many times.

Why does Wild Bill wear only one spur?

What does Wild Bill make with a hammer and a cracker?

He figures that if one side of his horse
    ran, the other would, too.
A crummy situation.

Annie O'Kay was sitting in a restaurant
when a man came in and ordered two
chocolate sundaes and a piece of apple pie
a la mode. She knew instantly that he
was a sailor. How?

And-Annie O'Kay and Wild Bill Hiccup
    want you to remember this:
    If everybody owned a horse, the world
    would be more stabilized.

He had a sailor suit on.

If everybody owned a horse,
the world would be more stable-ized!